A GUINEA PIG

Pride & Prejudice

A GUINEA PIG

Pride & Prejudice

A NOVEL
IN THREE VOLUMES

AN ADAPTATION OF THE ORIGINAL BY

JANE AUSTEN

LONDON
BLOOMSBURY PUBLISHING, BEDFORD SQUARE.
2015

CONTENTS

DRAMATIS PERSONAE

Elizabeth ∿ Molly

Mr. Darcy ∿ Hollie

Mr. Wickham ∿ Elsie

Mr. Bingley ∾ Billie

Mr. Collins ∾ Millie

Lady Catherine ∾ Guinnea

Lydia ∾ Doris

Jane ∾ Mabel

Mrs. Bennet ∾ Wilma

Netherfield Park

VOLUME ONE

t is a truth universally acknowledged, that a single man in possession of a good fortune, must be in want of a wife.

Netherfield Park had been taken by a certain
Mr. Bingley, a single man of large fortune;
four or five thousand a year.

Mrs. Bennet, who had five unmarried daughters, was greatly excited by the arrival of Mr. Bingley in the neighbourhood. By all accounts he was young, wonderfully handsome, extremely agreeable and, to crown the whole, he meant to be at the next ball.

To be fond of dancing was a certain step towards falling in love; and very lively hopes of Mr. Bingley's heart were entertained.

Jane

Elizabeth

Mary

Kitty

Lydia

'It is very likely that he may fall
in love with one of them.'

But at the ball it was his friend Mr. Darcy who soon drew the attention of the room by his fine, tall person, handsome features, noble mien; and the report which was in general circulation within five minutes after his entrance, of his having ten thousand a year and a large estate in Derbyshire.

Mr. Bingley was good looking, but Mr. Darcy was much handsomer, a fine figure of a man...

r. Darcy was looked at with great admiration for about half the evening, till he slighted Elizabeth Bennet by refusing to dance with her.

'She is tolerable,' he said, 'but not handsome enough to tempt *me.*'

He was the proudest, most disagreeable man in the world,
and every body hoped that he would never come there again.

But as their acquaintance grew over time, Mr. Darcy began to find that Elizabeth's face was rendered uncommonly intelligent by the beautiful expression of her dark eyes.

In fact, Darcy had never been so bewitched by any woman as he was by her. He really believed, that were it not for the inferiority of her connections, he should be in some danger.

What painter could do justice to those beautiful eyes?

et despite his burgeoning affection, Darcy soon found himself quarrelling with Elizabeth.

'*Your* defect,' said Elizabeth, 'is a propensity to hate every body.'

'And yours,' he replied, with a smile, 'is willfully to misunderstand them.'

Elizabeth found him proud and haughty, and Darcy wisely resolved that he would not even look at her.

By tea-time, however, it was clear that Mr. Bingley and Jane Bennet were in love.

Bingley was full of joy and attention for Jane;
he talked scarcely to any one else.

ome days later, the Bennets set off on a walk to Meryton with Mr. Collins, a visiting cousin who was eager to improve his acquaintance with Elizabeth.

'I am happy on every occasion,' Mr. Collins told Elizabeth, 'to offer those little delicate compliments which are always acceptable to ladies.'

hey were introduced to Mr. Wickham, who had come from town to accept a commission in the corps. He had all the best part of beauty – a fine countenance, a good figure, and a happy readiness of conversation.

*All were struck with the stranger's air,
all wondered who he could be.*

he party was increased by the unexpected arrival of Mr. Darcy and Mr. Bingley. Darcy was beginning to determine not to fix his eyes on Elizabeth, when they were suddenly arrested by the sight of Wickham.

Elizabeth, happening to see the countenance of both men as they looked at each other, was all astonishment at the effect of the meeting. Both changed colour; one looked white, the other red.

What could be the meaning of it?
It was impossible to imagine;
it was impossible not to long to know.

hen they chanced to be alone together, Mr. Wickham told Elizabeth the history of his acquaintance with Mr. Darcy.

'We played together as children,' he said. 'Mr. Darcy's father was my godfather, and bequeathed me the best living in his will, but when the living fell, Darcy gave it elsewhere.'

Wickham shook his head. 'Darcy was jealous of his father's uncommon attachment to me; pride has often been his best friend. The fact is, that we are very different sort of men, and that he hates me.'

'The greatest part of our youth was passed together;
inmates of the same house, sharing the same amusements...'

Elizabeth honoured Wickham for his noble refusal to expose Darcy's villainy to the world, and thought him handsomer than ever.

'Mr. Wickham is the most agreeable man I ever saw,' she thought. 'How am I to know that it would be wisdom to resist?'

But before she could think of marrying Wickham, Mr. Collins surprised her with a proposal of marriage!

'Nothing remains but for me to assure you in the most animated language of the violence of my affection.'

r. Collins was refused, though with no little difficulty. But he soon recovered, and married Elizabeth's best friend Charlotte, who was not at all romantic and only asked for a comfortable home.

Mrs. Bennet, however, was less phlegmatic.

'Miss Lizzy, if you take it into your head to go
on refusing every offer of marriage in this way,
you will never get a husband at all!'

The Parsonage

VOLUME TWO

ut all was quickly forgiven, and Elizabeth soon visited the new Mr. and Mrs. Collins at their parsonage home in Kent, where they were entertained by Lady Catherine de Bourgh.

Lady Catherine's manner of receiving them was not
such as to make her visitors forget their inferior rank.
The party did not supply much conversation.

he visit passed pleasantly enough till one day Elizabeth was suddenly roused by the sound of the door bell, and to her utter amazement, Mr. Darcy walked into the room and asked for her hand in marriage.

Elizabeth's astonishment was beyond expression, but Darcy's pride was still overbearing. He *spoke* of apprehension and anxiety, but he was sure of being accepted; he lingered on the inferiority of her family; in short, he behaved in a most ungentlemanlike manner. And how could she marry the man who had treated Mr. Wickham so infamously?

So she declined his offer.

'I had not known you a month before I felt that you were the last man in the world whom I could ever be prevailed upon to marry.'

But then Mr. Darcy wrote her a long letter, relating the truth about Mr. Wickham's wanton profligacy and his elopement with the fifteen-year-old Georgiana Darcy – Mr. Darcy's own sister – which Darcy had only thwarted at the very last moment.

A gamester!

he letter had quite an effect on Elizabeth Bennet's opinion of Mr. Darcy.

'How despicably have I acted!' Elizabeth cried. 'Had I been in love, I could not have been more wretchedly blind! Till this moment, I never knew myself.'

Pemberley

VOLUME THREE

lizabeth returned home to Hertfordshire. Her spirits were sadly affected and all sense of pleasure lost in shame, until her aunt and uncle, Mr. and Mrs. Gardiner, invited her to join them on their northern tour; she joyfully accepted.

The party arrived in Derbyshire – and as Mr. Darcy was away in town, Mrs. Gardiner decided they should visit his estate at Pemberley. Walking around the beautiful grounds and admiring the delightful aspects, Elizabeth everywhere saw Darcy's restrained yet elegant taste.

At that moment she felt that to be the mistress of Pemberley might be something!

ut Mr. Darcy had in fact returned to Pemberley unexpectedly early. Their eyes instantly met, and the cheeks of each were overspread with the deepest blush.

His behaviour was so strikingly altered; he had never spoken with such gentleness. She knew not what to think, nor how to account for it.

'Why is he so altered?' thought Elizabeth. 'From what can it proceed? It is impossible that he should still love me.'

ut her astonishment at Darcy's unaffected cordiality was rudely interrupted by a letter from Jane containing news of the most shocking kind.

Elizabeth's sister Lydia had eloped – with Wickham!

'There is nothing but love, flirtation and officers in Lydia's head. But she has no money, no connections, nothing that can tempt Wickham to marry her – she is lost forever.'

lizabeth returned to Longbourn immediately and waited for further news of her sister's predicament. Through her aunt, she discovered that Mr. Darcy had hunted Wickham down in London and induced him to marry Lydia. Darcy had also paid off Wickham's gambling debts and bought him a commission in a new regiment quartered in faraway Newcastle.

Elizabeth was stunned to learn of the pains he had taken, but her heart did whisper that he had done it for her.

A few weeks later, Darcy visited the Bennets at Longbourn with his friend Mr. Bingley, who had finally proposed to Jane.

[44]

'Good gracious!' cried Mrs. Bennet. 'If that disagreeable Mr. Darcy is not coming here again with our dear Bingley!'

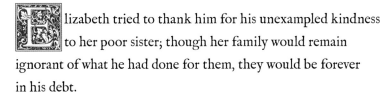lizabeth tried to thank him for his unexampled kindness to her poor sister; though her family would remain ignorant of what he had done for them, they would be forever in his debt.

'Your *family* owe me nothing,' Darcy said. 'Much as I respect them, I believe I thought only of *you*.'

They walked on, without knowing in what direction.
There was too much to be thought, and felt, and said,
for any attention to other objects.

This time Elizabeth accepted Fitzwilliam Darcy's proposal.

'I love him.'

And thus it was that she sat down to write to her aunt, Mrs. Gardiner:

I am the happiest creature in the world. Mr. Darcy sends
you all the love in the world that he can spare from me;
and you are all to come to Pemberley at Christmas.

Yours, &c.

Elizabeth Darcy

THE END

Small pets are abandoned every day, but the lucky ones end up in rescue centres where they can be looked after and rehomed.

You may not know it, but some of these centres are devoted entirely to guinea pigs. They work with welfare organizations to give first class advice and information, as well as finding loving new owners for the animals they look after.

If you've fallen a little bit in love with guinea pigs as well as with Mr. Darcy, perhaps think of supporting your local rescue centre!

The publishers would like to thank Amanda, Pauline and Jenn, as well as Jane, Charles, Caroline, Rosie, Phoebe and Alison, for their continuing comradeship and generosity. Thanks also to Belmondo for bringing this little book to life.

JANE AUSTEN was born in 1775 and went on to become one of the greatest novelists in English literature. Her work includes such perennial favourites as *Pride & Prejudice*, *Persuasion* and *Emma*, and has been adapted for radio, television and film.

TESS GAMMELL was born in 1987 and when she is not sewing miniature bonnets or welding tiny lamp posts, she works as a freelance set designer on a variety of scales for fashion, film, events and window displays. She lives in London.

ALEX GOODWIN was born in 1985 and when he is not hacking the work of a certain famous novelist into guinea-pig-friendly chunks, he writes his own fiction (which he hopes might one day receive the same treatment). He lives in London.

Bloomsbury Publishing
An imprint of Bloomsbury Publishing Plc

50 Bedford Square
London
WC1B 3DP
UK

1385 Broadway
New York
NY 10018
USA

www.bloomsbury.com

First published in Great Britain 2015

No animals died, were harmed or were placed under undue stress during the production of this publication. The publishers can confirm that the animals involved were treated with respect and that their owners were present throughout all photography shoots.

British Library Cataloguing-in-Publication Data
A catalogue record for this book is available from the British Library.

Library of Congress Cataloguing-in-Publication data has been applied for.

ISBN UK:
HB: 978-1-4088-6551-4
EPUB: 978-1-4088-6552-1

ISBN US:
HB: 978-1-63286-242-6
EPUB: 978-1-63286-243-3

2 4 6 8 10 9 7 5 3 1

Costume, props & illustration: Tess Gammell   Photography & book design: Belmondo

Printed and bound in China by C&C Offset Printing Co., Ltd

All papers used by Bloomsbury Publishing are natural, recyclable materials made from wood grown in well-managed forests. The manufacturing processes conform to the environmental regulations of the country of origin.